*Lovely
Endearments*

Lovely Endearments

LaQianya Huynh

AuthorHouse™
1663 Liberty Drive
Bloomington, IN 47403
www.authorhouse.com
Phone: 1-800-839-8640

© 2012 by LaQianya Huynh. All rights reserved.

No part of this book may be reproduced, stored in a retrieval system, or transmitted by any means without the written permission of the author.

Published by AuthorHouse   03/28/2012

ISBN: 978-1-4685-7208-7 (sc)
ISBN: 978-1-4685-7206-3 (hc)
ISBN: 978-1-4685-7207-0 (e)

Library of Congress Control Number: 2012905817

Any people depicted in stock imagery provided by Thinkstock are models, and such images are being used for illustrative purposes only.
Certain stock imagery © Thinkstock.

Because of the dynamic nature of the Internet, any web addresses or links contained in this book may have changed since publication and may no longer be valid. The views expressed in this work are solely those of the author and do not necessarily reflect the views of the publisher, and the publisher hereby disclaims any responsibility for them.

Contents

About The Author xi

My Love, My Soul 1
Anxiety in Asia 7
Birthday, Clouds 11
Café 12
Dearest God 14
Dorothy 17
He Was 18
In The Park 20
It is Your Birthday 22
Jeannie 25
Laura, Laura Pearl 26
Loving You, My Dream 28
My Daughter 30
My Love, My Wish 32
My Mother 35
My Son's Prayer 38
Night Song 42
Nurse 44
One Heart, One Mind 46

Pain	51
Run	53
Show Me	55
The Beggar	58
The Bold & Beautiful	61
The Day has Come	63
The Doctor	64
The Green Man	67
The Korean	70
The Music	71
The River and Bridge	74
The Road Back Home	76
The Streets	78
The Tree	80
This Christmas	82
Time to Heal	84
Vietnam	85
Yes You Are	88
You Are Part	90

Dedication

I dedicate this book to all who have inspired me to be the woman that I have become. Also, to those individuals who have found love, lost a great love or lover, and to those who have learned to love again.

Love Always,
LaQianya Huynh

About The Author

As an adolescent I wrote narratives, lyrics and ode prose. Yet, this book was mostly inspired by real life experiences, international travel, friends and family that I will never forget. In this book you will discover love and its various endearments through foreign words, dramatic monologues, ballads, and free verse prose. For the most part, romanticism text conveys my most deeply embedded thoughts. As you read, I hope that my words will enlighten your wonderful heart and calm your soul. Welcome to my world and always remember my motto: "Love from the heart makes you stronger!"

Enjoy!

My Love, My Soul

Feel me, know me, sense me, and fear me not. Don't be afraid of the unknown. Our souls are connected! Our hearts are intertwined by God's divine grace. I didn't ask for you, but somehow God lead me to you.

However, I ponder these thoughts: Do you know who or what you are? Is this a celestial intervention? Finally, is this Love and soul breakable?

I can answer them . . . and after many years I know now what love from the soul is . . . So let me tell you . . .

You are my soul mate. Sweetheart you know me, you sense my ever lively being in this vague world.

Sweetheart, fear me not for I am here for you always and forever. Most of all, you love me dearly, you like my quirky ways, and you understand me.

My love, God has heard our cries! His angels are always with us as we constantly fight Satan's demons. And, I am so glad he examined us . . . Also, I am most thankful for all he does in our lives . . . for he knew our purpose long before our mother's bestowed life on this wretched earth. However, God knows every ambition we appreciate in life. Yet, somehow adversity tries to impede on our success.

Sweetheart God has given me strength and he has nailed your trivial apocalypse to the wall and cast them down to the pits of Hell. Even now, he is mending and molding our broken hearts, broken promises, and unfinished goals. Most importantly, he even pardons our disobedience as our minds, bodies and souls grow closer to him.

Humbly, I declare this to you my darling, I stand before you boldly and proudly . . . for you are my greatest joy. You are precious to me. With all my might and strength that God has bestowed upon me . . . Sweetheart, I am simply going to love you wholeheartedly and thoroughly in my mind, with my lithe body, with my earthlike spunky soul and with my inner most sublime spirit.

My love, my heart swells just to think of you . . . My heart even races just to catch a glimpse of you. In its entirety, the touch of your lips and hair is so marvelous. Even listening to your voice, and seeing you as I touch you ever so lightly. Come a little closer and listen as I speak softly to you.

With faith and righteousness, our love will flourish and for a while time will stand still. My sweet love, never feel alone . . . For your soul mate awaits you patiently. She feels your anguish; she knows all of your hearts' desires. My love, we belong to one another. We are dearly kindred spirits here on earth. Our love is strong; it's bold and remarkably beautiful. Most of all, our souls are endearing and very tender that's extremely visible for any human eye abroad.

My sweet gentle giant, our love is here to stay. Your heart is so strong. So, please let the tenderness seep inside for a while . . . it wants to destroy your bewilderment and share that wondrous affection and pride that no other has ever captured before.

Sweetheart, I want to urge you, encourage you and give you all my suppressed love. It's dying to free it self. My love, this kind of adoration is very rare and it's very pure in its mold.
I can't wait to show you my entire being . . . my entire heart and soul that waits only for you.

My sweet love, when you feel alone. Simply close your eyes and feel the warm breeze and imagine my hand on your smooth face saying "I Love You" fondly. Sweetheart, always know that our love was created by God and that this love lasts an eternity for you are the love of my life and I am eternally grateful that I have found my soul mate here on earth.

Anxiety in Asia

Anxiety in Asia is a primal fear coupled with great disturbances of a perfectly sound mind . . .

No matter how brilliant or how useless, at any age or any given time.

Anxiety, without the proper treatment, will kill one's greatest hopes, dreams, and wondrous desires.

Why does this condition exist? Only God knows why!

Dearest god, anxiety is every where on this earth. Twenty-four hours a day . . . It never leaves them . . . it consistently nags and pulls at them.

All around the world, this dreadful condition rears its ugly head through its unknowing victim.

Again . . . Like magic it appears; you can see it in their faces, in their walk, in their talk, and hidden secretly in their voices . . . Why? I can not say for I am not the gatekeeper of their emotions.

Anxiety never dies for them. All their worries tacked on their backs . . . stretched across their faces . . . Minds weighing heavily in the darkness . . .

Look, there is a man in the distant crevice of the alley . . . his foot is missing; his face is disfigured more like erased from the depths of the Black Sea.

No matter the severity of this condition, they will carefully deny treatment!

One must save face instead of inhibiting sanity! What a great pity . . . My heart goes out to them . . . Still, I train my gaze on the wild woman and man on the bus . . . we watch each other closely . . . what will we say? What will we do? How should I react? Kindly, I smile and swiftly I walked away.

Birthday, Clouds

*Sweetheart the clouds are all around us . . .
Sometimes they are calm, but we have seen how tumultuous they can be.
Be that as it may, on this day, your birthday, the clouds are inactive; they are immobile on this beautiful day.
Sweetheart, the clouds trapped me in the midst of my madness . . . they showed me something wonderful. Years ago, those clouds caught a glimpse of something so sweet and innocent. You were created out of love for all to see. Wow! What a child you were . . . and now the clouds are still smiling upon us all . . . for you have the strongest of all hearts, you are the bravest of all men, and most of all you are just magnificent.
Happy Birthday Sweetheart!*

Café

Come with me.
See the river ahead?
It's a secluded Café along the river bank.
Let's go over there.
Take my hand, I will lead the way.
Please stand a little closer. Right here!
Do you smell that?
Something's amiss? Or maybe it's something deliciously floating in the air that I'm not accustomed to.
Dear God, touch my hot skin. Suddenly, the epidermis seems to be on fire!
Oh, right here, stop right here!
My charismatic lover . . .
Come; come much closer my dear love.
Breathe this enchanting air. After a mouthful . . . I do believe . . .

*We will gulp and pant long into the mid
summer night along this river's bank.
Please have a dance with me.
Sing with me along the river rocks of love.
And . . . tell me your darkest secrets.
With great anticipation, I always see your
handsome face staring back at me.
Those wonderful slanted brown eyes beckoning
me as they tranquilize my body.
Each time I must ask you too . . .
Release me and take me to that place again
with you.
And thereafter . . .
I shall take your hand and go with you to our
Café along the river rocks of love.*

Dearest God

Dearest God, how did you know that today
was my birthday?
How did you know that man and woman
would need each other so much?
Dearest God, you are a mystery.
You are the Alfa and the Omega to many loyal
worshipers.
Dearest God, how do we go on?
This world is so troubled and fed-up.

Faith and morality constantly battle with humans on earth daily.
Unfortunately, in this case, faith is misunderstood.
Dearest god, where did our spirit man go?
Let him . . . that spirit man rise up again, let the spirit man shine brightly through us.

*Dearest god, give us strength, guide us through this awful time.
Dearest god, our flesh, our minds and our souls are weakened by Satan's wrath. Dearest God, hold us, mend us, and bring us closer to you because we need you. For today was another birthday on this
troubled earth.*

Dorothy

Dorothy is a woman of grace.
Dorothy is a woman of tender love.
Dorothy has a heart of gold.
Dorothy, you are special to me.
Dorothy has a smile like no other.
Dorothy listens and she cares.
Dorothy shines like the moon.
Dorothy is my sweet friend for life.
Dorothy you are truly unforgettable.

He Was

He was my king

He was a splendid mystery to me

He was the athletic one

He was a charming one

He was my world as a little girl

He was a fashionable chap

He was there . . . he was here . . . he was everywhere

He was a hard working American . . . my American Idol

He was the driver of the bluest Monte Carlo

He was a fish swimming in the sea . . . the black tuna that melted

He was a football player mastering a touchdown on his field

He was a track runner on his mark . . . yes he was the man I will never forget

He was my dad

In The Park

In the park you will find me
Laying on my back gazing into the bluest of
blue skies
And . . .
As I smile
I feel your presence
I want . . . and
I will draw silly shapes and holy apparitions'
with cumulus clouds
As . . .
My soul skips in the wind
It's so peaceful here
That . . .
Even the wind makes a way through my thick
mane

Lovely Endearments

Some how . . .
I still feel your presence
Then again, you are everywhere and my heart
is filled with joy and love
If only
I . . .
Could breathe in your essence
My world would outshine the farthest orbital
planet in the Milky Way
Oh come ye be faithful
Joyful and triumphant on this beautiful day
And . . .
Bask in this amorous light.

It is Your Birthday

Years ago a little baby was born. This little child was conceived out of sheer love and copious joy. What a blessing he is, what a blessing she is, what a blessing they are . . . children of the world . . . Smile children it's your birthday!

Many children were born on this wonderful day. Can you recall this day? Well, no one can voice that answer. However, it was the day that you opened your eyes for the first time. It was the first day that you were able to feel, taste, smell and even see outside your mother's womb. Because of your mother's devine love and care, you are with us now.

Smile children, today is your birthday! Take in this time, go to the beach or even go to the lake and soak up the sun's ultraviolent rays. Then, open your eyes and breathe in deeply for you have just made it another year!

Jeannie

Jeannie is my rock
Jeanie is my best female friend
Jeanine changes like the wind
Jeannie is fine like wine
Jeannie will make you work
Jeannie will teach you all about life
Jeannie is the greatest humanitarian of all time
Jeannie is smart, not a tart
Jeannie is eclectic, yet she is eccentric
Jeannie loves all creeds and races . . . so
If you are a lost soul Jeannie will make you whole again.

Laura, Laura Pearl

Laura is one of my greatest loves of life

Laura is a breath of fresh air

Laura is greatly respected and adored by many

Laura listens

Laura Pearl will fire her loose cannon when you are least expected

Laura Pearl will make you laugh

Laura Pearl will make your cry

Laura Pearl will put you in your rightful place

Laura will walk far and wide to accomplish her chore

Laura will make you melt when you try that chewy cake

Laura . . . Laura Pearl I love you so

Loving You, My Dream

Loving you produces tears of joy. This love, in all of its uniqueness and improbable chances is exceptionally pure. Be that as it may, in my dream, I was at the gala dancing. Then, suddenly, I noticed a man with great character, diligence, and subtle beauty beam as he focused on a beautiful woman across the room. This was a match made from heaven. Love formed straight from the heart and the soul. Their lives at that moment were complete and all the others were obsolete. It wasn't until that moment, in this dream. I realized what loving you really means.

Loving you brings joy to my life. Loving you makes life worth living. My love for you grows more and more each day that we live here on this earth. Loving you is sweet, it's kind, it's divine, and most of all its everlasting.

My dearest love, I am here for you always and forever. Always, keep in mind that your troubles are my troubles and your happiness means my happiness. Some how my love, we will fight the woes of the world together. Because loving you makes life so grand and most exciting even in my dream.

My Daughter

My daughter is unique . . . the eyes of her grandmother . . . Yes, she has them . . . the body of an Asian/ Greek goddess . . . As a baby, my daughter never blinked an eye . . . she always watched . . . her eyes transfixed on her target . . . her subject of concern.

My daughter's mind is brilliant; it grows and manifests all things that it can possibly capture. My daughter will change the world.

*My daughter will always be a part of me . . .
In my sweet heart, in my lovely soul . . . in
my glorious body. My daughter will conquer
all . . . My daughter will love all who loves her
dearly.*

*My daughter will cry if you are to hurt her.
However, she will never forget your wrong
doings . . .*

*My daughter will love you still because she is
of her mother and of her grandmother and of
her great-grandmother.*

My Love, My Wish

My love my wish is to be with you

My love is waiting right here for you

You are the light in my life

That brings me joy every day

The sun is shining on my emollient face

Come with me . . . Now

Feel me . . . Smell all of me . . . Touch all of me . . . Everywhere

The light of day is upon us

Leading the way to our private never land

My love is . . . Right here for you my Sweet Darling

Come now . . . And

Catch a glimpse of our future right here on this exciting . . . Yet

Refreshing beach

My love is searing right here on this delightful beach

Waiting for you . . .

Right here . . .

My love just swells every day . . .

With frantic anticipation

Knowing

I will feel your soft hands touching mine again.

My Mother

My mother is beautiful

My mother is the new mother Theresa

My mother loves you

My mother cares about you

My mother has the patience of Jobe

My mother will guide you in your time of need

My mother will protect you

My mother will even scold you at any given age

My mother will punish you for all your wrong doings

My mother is sweet by her own right

My mother has many admirers

My mother is warm by heart

My mother is tender

My mother is the best of all mothers

Most of all, my mother will always love you

My Son's Prayer

My son is wise beyond his years . . .

My son is wild in his young life

My son has no fear of danger

He is the fabulous dare devil of all time.

My son is magnificent, he is aggressive . . .

My son has the drive and great ambitions of life just like the Vietnamese.

He is of his father and of his mother's likeness

*My son has grown into a young man . . .
Where did the time go?*

Just yesterday, he was a tiny babe in my arms.

Constantly, demanding my milk, my heart, and my tender soul that I gave to him . . . My son

My son is handsome.

All the girls, young women, and even some men adore him.

I pray to thee . . . to guide my son. Guide his heart, for many of his admires mean no good . . . Let my son distinguish the sheep and wolfs in his path.

Lord, I pray that he grows into his name . . .

He is my chosen son . . . he is the strongest of all men . . . He is and always will be the bravest of all men.

*My son will show them all . . . he will deliver
life one day . . .*

*My son will learn to be a tender lover to the
one mate he chooses . . .*

*My son, never fear, I am always near;
however far you or I may go.*

*I will always be in your heart forever and
ever always.*

Night Song

In the night we are wild and free as we listen to the night song play. As the night song plays out into the world... children, men and women dance about their living rooms. Teenagers are sneaking around their parent's backs, young adults are dating about the town and troublemakers are doing their dirty deeds.

Tonight as your night song plays, you are enthralled for a brief moment. Slowed with apparitions from the past, all those suppressed child hood memories seeping into your conscious mind. Time just fades away as we age... must we forget those lovely times... those horrid times and all those dynamic frills of life?

Oh night song! Sing loudly for me! Free them; free all illusions of the past . . . set my soul a fire . . . set my soul free . . . give me peace . . . give us all your Divine power.

Take us to a higher plane . . . Take us to the depth of your deepest sea . . . Then, take us to the highest mountain peak as my night song plays loudly into the midnight hour. By Golly, I will sing and dance way into the night. Because I am free! My soul was freed . . . Love has appeared, my body is warm to touch and my heart has doubled in size again. My lovely reader, sing and dance as your night song lives on and on.

Nurse

Nurse show me the way to heaven

Nurse my feeble body here on earth

Oh nurse . . . my mind is so heavy

Nurse my body is so weak and tired of this tremendous pain

Nurse show me the way . . . to that peaceful place

Nurse me back to the day that I died

Nurse show me my day of birth

Nurse . . . Set my soul free . . . show me the joy in my parent's eyes

Nurse show me how to right all my wrong doings

Nurse me back to my life . . . and I will love to live once again

One Heart, One Mind

We are one heart

We are one mind

Your thoughts are with me . . . Oh yes . . .
Inhale deeply . . . As

Your thoughts continue to lead me some . . .
Where . . . Some . . . How . . .

Your heart even found me in Paris . . . ô! . . .
Oui Monsieur!

Your lovely heart even found me . . . In . . .

*Bangkok, Thailand saying "hello my love" . . .
But then . . .*

As I walked through the terminal in Korea

You were in my peculiar mind . . .

Then,

I noticed my heart skipped its typical beat

As a consequence, I felt its euphoric malleable
drum . . . Then . . .

Instantly . . .

My mind was literally gone . . . Where could it
possibly be? . . . It's . . .

In a daze . . . In a misty daze . . . Some iffy
phase . . . Oh it's defined as . . .

A cozy haze of love . . .

Some . . . Where . . . Some . . . How

My mind and heart is within you

Some . . . Where on the elongated Pacific Ocean

Even . . . As you timidly swam to the depths of the Black Sea . . .

Trepidation lost its shallow home . . .
However . . .

*In lieu of this distinctive moment, I am . . .
Truly on cloud nine*

Jovial some may say . . .

*Just knowing that my mind and my heart
reside in you*

Placates cavernous affections . . .

Because . . .

We are one heart and one mind.

Pain

Pain hurts

Pain burns the core of you

This pain propels the sickest of psychopaths

This pain even serves the outlandish terrorists of our world

Pain comes from all walks of life

Pain doesn't discriminate

Pain has no care of its target

Is pain a measure of intense tolerance?

Pain is a powerful teacher

This kind of pain binds us in the oddest way

Pain could be a vicious cycle

If you let it come and go

Fight this pain and hold your ground

Stand your ground and defend your right to survive this pain that binds

the core of you

Run

Run wild

Run free

Run until the sun doesn't shine

Run to the moon

Run for love and a dove

Run into the broom in your room

Oh! Just run for the sake of running

Run to the plane

Run to Spain

Run to the state of Maine, but don't forget to run from the fire flame

Show Me

Show me the way to your heart

Show me that pure and innocent love

Show me the way . . .

I have lost my way to your heart

Oh what a peculiar day

On that particular day I was sightless by an overwhelming glow

*Show me that magnificent masculine vision
over and over again.*

*Perhaps, it was just a figment of my
mysterious subconscious mind*

*That feverish, tainted subconscious mind that
never sleeps and leaps about the room*

Oh, show me the way to my love

Now show me the way to your heart

Love is the way to my heart

Show me the way to that place

Oh show me the way to your heart

My love is right here, right here for you

My darling . . . my dove . . . My dearest love of all . . .

Show me the way to your heart!

The Beggar

Day in, day out the beggars will come . . . No matter the place . . . they will come . . .

The beggar is old, the beggar is middle aged . . . the beggar is a baby just out of its mother's belly.

On the ferry boat, in the hospital, in the Supper Market, and in the Café the beggar will find you. The beggar is blind; he or she is bold in their fold.

The beggar is 92 years old . . . her back is hurting . . . her leg is limp . . . I feel her pain . . . This agony she is in . . . Her face has a rippled print from the sun . . . as the ferry comes she cries loudly . . . Help me! Help me! Give me! Give me!

The 92 year old beggar wants to die . . . her eyes told me that . . . her body screamed to me . . . her eyes were daunting, but there were years of hurt in her golden eyes.

*Oh! My lord I pray to thee . . . Keep her safe
from harm . . . this beggar.*

*Perhaps, years ago she was a glorious one . . .
What happened to her? Who did this to her?
No one knows . . .*

*Day in, day out the beggar feeds on you
and me! . . . My soft hearted love of God and
humanity goes out to all . . . Still, I pray
today . . . for the beggar will always live on.*

The Bold & Beautiful

The bold is the light of day.

The beauty is you!

The boldness of your voice . . . stops me . . . wraps me in a fog that holds me so still.

Your face . . . the bold one . . .

Makes me fall into a deep slumber of desire

The slumber that says you are bold and you are very

beautiful to me.

The light that shines in your eyes drives me wild... makes me want and need you so much

The light in your eyes tell me all things.

There's no need for words... because

your eyes are very bold and beautiful to me.

The Day has Come

The day has come for you to fly high in the sky

The day has come for you to rise up

The day has come for you to give birth

The day has come for life to deliver its feast

The time has come for you to file your tile

They day has come for the captain to set his sail

The day has come for us to prevail

The Doctor

The doctor cares

The doctor will not discriminate

The doctor is responsible for you and for me

The doctor is said to be your human god on earth

The doctor will repair your backbone

The doctor will mold dentures for your teeth and build prosthetic legs and arms if you are disabled.

On the contrary, can the doctor mend a broken heart?

Does the doctor know it . . . how did it fail . . . how did the heart weaken when the heart was disease free? Doctor, my dear Doctor tell me how to solve this mystery.

Oh doctor, you are the one who knows all . . . in time . . .

The doctor will save your life if you let him or her.

The doctor will bring you great joy.

However, the doctor may bring you sadness . . . Beware of the doctor.

The redhead doctor will make your head spin.

The doctor will even uncover a new way of life in the future . . . who knows . . . just wait and see what the doctor has in store for you.

The Green Man

The green man is resilient

The green man has raw emotions

The green man loves and he hates like no other

The green man found me after many years

The green man changed my view of love and life

We are of the same culture

Yet, we have congruent clothing styles and diverse life styles

The green man is awfully tall

The green man is so lean and too viral for his own good

The green man gives pleasure like no other

Even now, the green man shows no emotion

The green man has a past that one can not ignore

The green man found me in my dream.

Why did you come? I have no clue.

Maybe the green man has found peace and solace in my pleasant dream

The Korean

In Korea you will find a yielding mystery.

The people . . . they live . . . they work . . . they are firm as they walk . . . the Korean is talented. In the female Korean you will discover a stoic, proud, and poised woman. Even the men . . . they are dignified in their traditional dress code.

The Korean smiles gently to others . . . the Korean frowns upon others . . . that is if you are a paying customer . . . it doesn't matter if you are flying, driving, swimming or crying the Korean will gladly take your money.

The Music

Listen as the music moves you, takes you to the highest plane. I feel every note as the piano pangs ... and pangs away. The music offers innovative soul, it breeds on its bridges and pelts on its breaks.

Hear the music! Feel this unusual sensation, feel the vibrations as the beat moves on to your skin, seeps into your subcutaneous tissue and pulls you down deeply through your cephalic veins. Suddenly, the music reaches your arterial arteries. This music nearly stops the heart for its power holds you captive. The music is breathtaking ... the music relaxes me as I fade into the late night.

Listen to the music; it is so clear that an alien's ear will turn to capture its essence. Do you feel it? . . . This unusual sensation that suddenly beats through you; regardless of its possessive power, the music is so soft now that it touches you oddly. Do you feel it? Do you feel the beat as the melody plays? The music moves through your body . . . dance . . . it says . . . dance with me . . . sway with me . . . And gently sway toward the sky.

Look up to the heavens and reach for the clouds above. Observe the luminous lights as the music moves you closer, as it delivers your troubled soul.

Dance, I say on to you my child, my sweet lover, my friends and even my enemies. Dance until you feel the rhythm. Let this wonderful music show you, enlighten you, hold you and simply take you in. For the music will consume you and hold you dearly.

The River and Bridge

This river brings life to its people.

Even so, this river flows into my heart.

After fifteen days of travel, I heard the river sing. It even told a short story as I sat and gazed about. Day after day, the people walk and ride across the river and its bridges.

I should not swim in it, for this river seems unclean. Perhaps, many years ago, this river was pure and pristine like its originator. As I observed the bridge's many white lowly arched bridges and softly lit white lights that even accommodated the dullest of spectacled eyes. At night, this river was so gorgeous and inviting.

Be that as it may, the river flows south and westward coupled with many sashes and ashes with fishing boats afloat.

Yet, this river exudes romance for lovers young and old. Across the river bank, I saw a young man and female together. They gently touched each other's faces and slowly moved into a smoldering kiss. I saw them from afar, as if I was right in there in front of them.

I can still see that special light in his eyes and the fire from her veneer . . . that . . . This was truly that undeniable young and blissful love.

Someday soon, I will return to this precise mark and find my yielding heart on this river and bridge that flows directly beyond my bewitched, un-betrothed and bewildered heart.

The Road Back Home

The road back home beckons me

The road back home takes me to that warm place

The road back home reminds me of my younger days in the rice fields

The road back home comforts my soul

The road back home gives me a peace of mind

The road back home knows that you are there waiting gaily.

The road back home stirs many emotions

The proverbial road back home knows my heart so well

Now the road back home is just a road that leads me back to home to you.

The Streets

The streets are busy . . .

The streets are wild with its daily patrons

The streets are rough in some parts, but extremely dangerous for one like me.

The streets, how wild it would be to rouse him in this place? . . . In this wild and busy street . . . right in the open view of the street's alley . . . those carnal urges . . . I must fight them for now because he is too shy in the streets . . . and even I for that matter . . . Have I lost my mind in the streets?

On the contrary, I am not afraid! I love a great challenge. I have seen many terrors in my young days . . . even encountered hundreds of thrills in my prime.

The streets are so tempting . . . lets run far away in the streets

Let's merge with those blinking lights

Let's sink in that whole over there, just over the pole

The streets grabbed me . . . but I can not be nabbed

For the streets have taught me well.

The Tree

The tree gives life

The tree yields the air we breathe

The tree gives us shelter . . . Oh my, I command this tree . . .

So, I ask this tree to protect me from those ultraviolent rays . . . because the sun was burning my face until the rain began . . . and then . . .

The leaves of this magnificent tree, folded delicately to catch the chilled rain from my face.

The tree shifts with the wind

The tree sways as the wind pushes the branches to its breaking point

The tree is very strong; I love this magnificent tree

The tree is rooted to its enormous protector for nourishment

Behold the tree was made by god and it will grow on and on as seasons change.

This Christmas

This Christmas welcome your family and your friends . . . for . . .

This Christmas your life will be renewed with blessings bestowed from the heavens above!

This Christmas my love with be with you . . .

This Christmas my children will grow one step higher and I will get a little wiser.

This Christmas, my friends will sing my favorite Christmas carol. As we swing with the highest king and waltz with the gallant of faults. This Christmas will be the best of all.

This Christmas my love will find you near the fire place . . . as I say

Happy Holidays to you and to all . . .

Time to Heal

Today is a beautiful day!

This is a time for you to heal.

Enjoy this time for God has a task in store for you.

Relax as your wondrous mind and your lithe body heals

This is a day of reflection.

A day of tender loving care . . .

A day of love that extends from me to you . . .

This is your time to heal!

Vietnam

Discover new life

Discover profound love

Discover your distant soul in Vietnam

Walk with me, Talk with me

In this language . . . in this beautiful place . . .
Vietnam

What a tropical place! . . . You can see the rain, the heat, and the steamy mist rise from the streets and to the greenest of rice fields.

Even so, you can feel your lovely body take in this life . . .

Then, the tension sets in . . . The drive of the old people verses the ambitious young and middle aged brewing as they compete to survive.

In Vietnam, you will find a new life and love of family.

My sweet reader, In Vietnam this profound love of life breeds . . . it even swells in a broken heart!

For all who know me, those who can feel me, touch me, and sense my lively being . . . through me . . .

You, my lovely reader will see this exotic land . . . as we ride on the Xe-Honda, as we walk on the streets of L.A., and fly over the Rocky Mountains . . . We will feel the life; feel the wind on our skin as we grin from ear to ear. Smile with me, laugh with me, and even cry with me because you have just discovered a new and profound you in Vietnam.

Yes You Are

You are strong!

You are brave!

Yes you are my friend!

You are wise for your age.

You are my ultimate lover.

You are simply you.

No one can replace you.

You are magnificent!

You are a man of intelligence!

You are living life on your terms.

No one could ever measure up to you.

Because you are loved by your family and friends . . .

Most of all, you are dearly loved by me.

Simply because you are amazing to me!

Yes You Are!

You Are Part II

You are my friend

You are my sweetest lover of all time

You are in my mind... in my heart... and in my glorious soul.

You are every woman's wish

Your mind is brilliant

You are intelligent

You are always in my dreams...

You are like silk . . . so smooth

You are afraid of my beauty . . . Yet, I am not afraid of yours

You are most exotic and very handsome

You are here and you are there and now you are everywhere

You are the prefect one for me.

❧ Lovely Endearments ❧

I hope that my words have enlightened your heart and have calmed your inner spirit to embrace love and life when it seems impossible. Welcome to my world and always remember my motto: "Love from the heart makes you stronger!"

Made in the USA
Lexington, KY
07 May 2013